Ripley's
Believe It or Not!®

Developed and produced by Ripley Publishing Ltd

This edition published and distributed by:

Mason Crest
450 Parkway Drive, Suite D, Broomall, PA 19008
www.masoncrest.com

Printed and bound in the United States of America

First printing
9 8 7 6 5 4 3 2 1

Ripley's Believe It or Not!
Animal Stories
ISBN: 978-1-4222-2771-8 (hardback)
ISBN: 978-1-4222-2788-6 (paperback)
ISBN: 978-1-4222-9032-3 (e-book)
Ripley's Believe It or Not!—Complete 8 Title Series
ISBN: 978-1-4222-2769-5

Cataloging-in-Publication Data on file with the Library of Congress

PUBLISHER'S NOTE
While every effort has been made to verify the accuracy of the entries in this book, the
Publishers cannot be held responsible for any errors contained in the work. They would
be glad to receive any information from readers.

WARNING
Some of the stunts and activities in this book are undertaken by experts and should not
be attempted by anyone without adequate training and supervision.

Ripley's Believe It or Not!®

Enter If You Dare

ANIMAL STORIES

www.MasonCrest.com

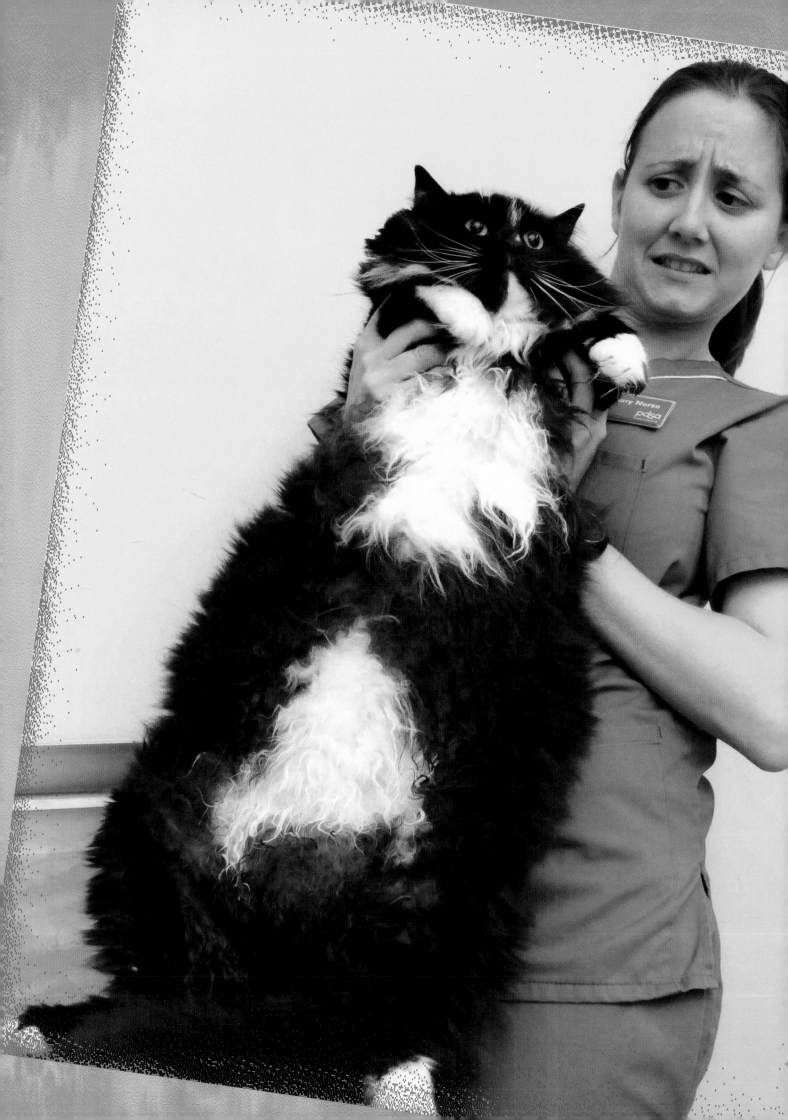

ANIMAL STORIES

Curious creatures. Discover
tail-waggingly fun animal features.
Meet the lady who lives with wild
animals, the racing pigs, and the
boy who keeps a 16-ft (4.9-m)
python as a pet!

Socrates the cat weighs 22 lb (10 kg),
double his ideal weight, so he has joined a
fat-fighting club for overweight animals...

Ripley's Revealed

flea CIRCUS

QUEEN OF THE FLEAS

MARIA FERNANDA CARDOSO, AN ARTIST FROM COLOMBIA, HAS MADE HER CAREER EXPLORING THE PHYSICAL CAPABILITIES OF ANIMALS—AND HER FAMOUS CARDOSO FLEA CIRCUS PROJECT IS NO EXCEPTION. IN 1996, CARDOSO SET UP A BIG TOP TENT, MADE BY THE FABRIC WORKSHOP AND MUSEUM IN PHILADELPHIA, AND TWO OTHER ARENAS FOR HER FLEA PERFORMERS TO USE. HER TROOP CONSISTED OF FLEA TRAPEZE ARTISTS, WIRE-WALKERS, AND FLEAS SHOT OUT OF CANNONBALLS. CARDOSO LEADS HER FLEAS, WHILE WEARING HER CIRCUS ATTIRE, THROUGH STUNTS THAT ARE DESIGNED TO TEST THEIR RESPONSES TO HEAT, LIGHT, AND CARBON DIOXIDE. ONCE THE FLEAS HAVE PERFORMED, THEY ARE REWARDED WITH HALF AN HOUR OF HER BLOOD.

The big top tent for Maria's Cardoso Flea Circus in Philadelphia.

One of her well-trained fleas balancing on a tightrope with a pole.

Flea-tastic Facts!

- A flea can pull up to 160,000 times its own weight; that's the same as a human pulling 3,900 school buses.
- There are at least 2,000 different species of flea.
- Fleas are thought to have been sucking blood for more than 100 million years.
- A flea can jump 200 times its own length; that's the same as a human jumping to the top of the Empire State Building.
- The largest infestation of fleas recorded was approximately 133,378,450 on a U.K. pig farm in 1986.
- A flea can produce up to 500 offspring in its lifetime.

A female cat flea tows a 19th-century cart in Germany at a circus.

Ripley's ask

Andy Clark is a flea-circus expert, and tells us why fleas really are the best performers in the world...

When was the first flea circus created?

Jewelers first used fleas when, after making smaller and smaller gold chains, someone had the idea of harnessing a flea to a chain. There are reports of chained fleas throughout the 1500s and 1600s and of fleas pulling miniature carriages as early as 1745. The man who is credited with making flea circuses popular as a performance in its own right is Louis Bertolotto, who performed with his "Educated Fleas" in London's Regent Street from around 1830, before touring the world with his act.

What is it about fleas that make them good circus performers?

Fleas have very strong legs and good balance. They can be harnessed with a wire loop around their neck like an ox's yoke. Once harnessed, they can then pull weights much larger than their own body mass. Fleas are good at tightrope walking and their strong legs can also be put to use kicking balls in miniature football matches. This does not harm the fleas, but their lifespan is not long, so a performer needs to regularly replace his fleas.

How can you learn to train fleas for your very own circus?

The training is really a process of selection. Some fleas don't take well to being harnessed and refuse to feed once enslaved. Some fleas are oversensitive to noise and lights, others are docile and not well suited to performing. However, many fleas just love walking around pulling chariots or kicking balls, so these are the ones that are used in performances.

The Alberti Flea Circus

The long-running, family-owned Alberti Flea Circus first opened in North Carolina in 1880. The current impresario is Jim Alberti, who learned how to train fleas from his grandfather at the age of 12.

Famous Fleas

William Heckler started his flea circus in New York in 1900 with his son Roy at the forefront by 1925. When World War II restricted his intake of fleas, Roy started breeding his own. As circus director of fleas, Roy would regularly feed his little performers with his own blood, allowing them to help themselves to his "quality human blood" and perform to their maximum potential. Choosing to breed females over males, as they are twice the size, Heckler would train them using a horizontal glass tube to walk or crawl instead of jump. Once they had hit their head a few times, they knew to stay low!

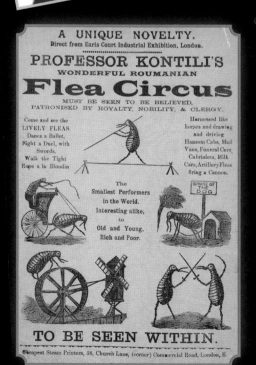

A UNIQUE NOVELTY.
Direct from Earls Court Industrial Exhibition, London.

PROFESSOR KONTILI'S
WONDERFUL ROUMANIAN

Flea Circus

MUST BE SEEN TO BE BELIEVED,
PATRONISED BY ROYALTY, NOBILITY, & CLERGY.

Come and see the
LIVELY FLEAS
Dance a Ballet,
Fight a Duel, with
Swords,
Walk the Tight
Rope a la Blondin

Harnessed like
horses and drawing
and driving
Hansom Cabs, Mail
Vans, Funeral Cars,
Cabriolets, Milk
Cars, Artillery Fleas
firing a Cannon.

The
Smallest Performers
in the World.
Interesting alike,
to
Old and Young,
Rich and Poor.

BEWARE OF
THE DOG

TO BE SEEN WITHIN.

Cheapest Steam Printers, 38, Church Lane, (corner) Commercial Road, London, E.

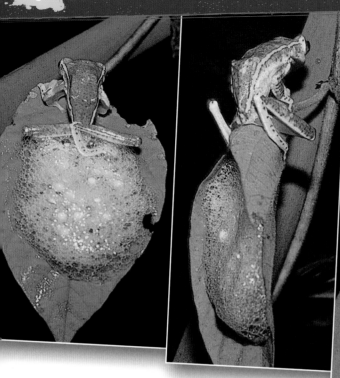

℞ BUNNY BOOM

In June 2009, Nancy Haseman of Rio Rancho, New Mexico, was found to be keeping 334 rabbits in her garden. She said her husband rescued a rabbit 12 years earlier after a neighbor abandoned it, then the couple began rescuing more rabbits. She had tried to keep the males separate from the females but the males kept hopping the fence.

℞ IN A SPIN

A seven-week-old kitten survived in July 2009 after being trapped in a washing machine for a full cycle, including a spin. Toby is believed to have crawled into the machine at his home in Aberdeenshire, Scotland, before it was switched on, in an attempt to escape the summer heat wave.

℞ REST PERIOD

Groundhogs breathe only once every five minutes during periods of hibernation.

℞ PAW CHOICE

Domestic cats can be either left-handed or right-handed, according to their sex. Particularly when faced with difficult tasks, females prefer to use their right paw while tom cats tend to use their left paw.

℞ MOTHER HEN

A hen in China adopted two orphaned puppies after their mother died. Owner Cao Fengying of Jiashan said the hen was best friends with the mother dog, and then looked after the puppies, fighting off other chickens who were trying to steal the puppies' food.

℞ EXTRA HEAD

In July 2009, a baby cow was born at a farm in Rivera, Colombia, with two heads but only one brain. The weight of the extra head meant the calf—named Jennifer—could not stand without help, so farmer Marino Cabrera built a sling to support her.

℞ FROG WEDDING

Two frogs were married in a solemn ceremony in the western Indian state of Maharashtra in June 2009 in an attempt to bring on delayed monsoon rains. Tradition says that if frogs are married off with full Vedic or Hindu rituals, the rain god is pleased and the heavens will open within days.

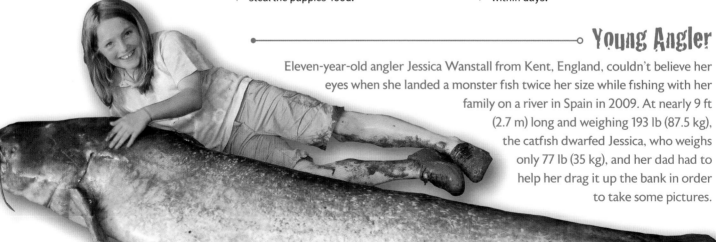

Young Angler

Eleven-year-old angler Jessica Wanstall from Kent, England, couldn't believe her eyes when she landed a monster fish twice her size while fishing with her family on a river in Spain in 2009. At nearly 9 ft (2.7 m) long and weighing 193 lb (87.5 kg), the catfish dwarfed Jessica, who weighs only 77 lb (35 kg), and her dad had to help her drag it up the bank in order to take some pictures.

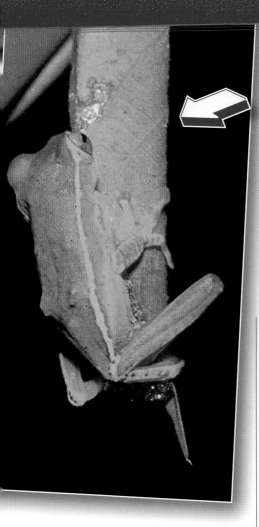

Frog's Eggs

Dr. S.D. Biju of the University of Delhi has discovered the ingenious method by which a type of Indian tree frog protects its young. The female frog carefully wraps its frogspawn in a leaf to make a foam-sealed container that prevents the embryos from drying out in the sunlight, then leaves them to develop on their own.

℞ DOLLAR NEST
A mouse made its home inside an ATM at a gas station in La Grande, Oregon, building its nest from 16 chewed-up $20 bills.

℞ FISH FAST
In some species of whalefish, the males stop eating entirely as they mature, their jaws waste away, and they live exclusively on energy stored in their massive, fatty liver.

℞ WINGED CAT
Born perfectly normal, a long-haired white cat in Chongqing, China, began sprouting winglike growths on either side of his spine when he was a year old. Some experts believe the bony "wings" are a freak mutation in the form of a Siamese twin growing inside the cat. Others think the cause may be genetic, the result of chemicals absorbed during his mother's pregnancy.

℞ FLUSHED AWAY
A pet goldfish survived being flushed down a toilet in East Kilbride, Scotland, and was eventually rescued from a sewage plant. The fish was put down the toilet because its owners thought it was dying, but it revived as it made its way through the town's underground waste water network and was spotted flailing about on a mesh filtering screen at the Scottish Water sewage site.

℞ LOST DEER
While fishing in Chesapeake Bay, Chad Campbell from Washington state and Bo Warren from Virginia found a whitetail deer swimming in 80 ft (25 m) of deep water 1.5 mi (2.4 km) from the nearest coast.

℞ ROLE REVERSAL
Although toads are normally the prey of venomous snakes, some mountain toads in Qingcheng Mountain Park, Sichuan, China, have turned nature on its head by eating one of their chief predators, Jerdon's pit vipers.

℞ WHEEL TRAP
An inquisitive cat that poked its head into the wheel of a car had to be rescued by firefighters after becoming stuck in the small hole in the center. Using specialist cutting gear, it took fire crews from Bury St Edmunds in Suffolk, England, an hour to free Casper the Siamese.

℞ DRINKING HABIT
The thorny devil lizard from Australia drinks water through its feet. Using cracks in its scales, it can absorb water through its feet and into its body.

℞ WINNING STREAK
Bertie the Labrador dog won his owner Dave Hallett from Sussex, England, $300 in a pub lottery five weeks in a row, beating odds of 282-million-to-one. He predicted the winning bonus ball by putting his nose up to a number on a board.

℞IPLEY'S RESEARCH

COMPARED TO OTHER CREATURES, IT IS RELATIVELY COMMON (ALTHOUGH STILL RARE) FOR BEARDED DRAGONS TO BE BORN WITH TWO HEADS IN CAPTIVITY. THIS MAY BE OWING TO INBREEDING AND THE FACT THAT PET BEARDED DRAGONS CAN PRODUCE LARGE NUMBERS OF EGGS EACH YEAR. TWO-HEADED DRAGONS HAVE TWO SEPARATE BRAINS, BUT CAN OFTEN COORDINATE THEIR BODY SURPRISINGLY WELL.

HEADS AND TAIL

FRANK AND BARBARA WITTE OF FRESNO, CALIFORNIA, HAVE A HIGHLY UNUSUAL PET. THEIR BEARDED DRAGON, ZAK-N-WHEEZIE, HAS TWO NAMES BECAUSE IT WAS BORN WITH TWO HEADS. EXPERTS PREDICTED THAT THE LIZARD WOULD NOT LIVE FOR LONG, BUT ZAK-N-WHEEZIE IS STILL GOING STRONG AND IS POSSIBLY THE LONGEST LIVING TWO-HEADED BEARDED DRAGON IN THE WORLD.

Rat-busters

The famous exterminator shop Julien Aurouze & Co, located on the rue des Halles in Paris, France, has always specialized in pest control or, more specifically, catching and killing rats. Founded in 1872, the shop window gives an obvious explanation of what they do, with stuffed rats hanging from traps by their mouths, and taxidermied rats scattered all over the displays inside.

R FALSE FOOT

A three-year-old Asian elephant whose front left foot was caught in a trap is able to walk again after he was fitted with a prosthetic foot. After cutting away 5 in (12 cm) of infected tissue, surgeons in Cambodia made a cast of Chhouk's stump so that a false foot could be created by a prosthetics team. He needed no anesthetic while the limb was being attached—just a steady supply of turnips and bananas.

R VENOMOUS MAMMAL

The *Hispaniolan solenodon*, a small mammal from Haiti and the Dominican Republic, is one of only a couple of mammals that has a venomous bite.

R MUSICAL ELEPHANT

An elephant at an English safari park entertains keepers and visitors by playing the harmonica. Five, a female African elephant at West Midlands Safari Park, discovered the harmonica after it was accidentally left on the side of her enclosure and soon learned to place the instrument in her trunk and blow out to produce some notes.

R GENTLE GIANT

Sancho, a longhorn steer from a farm in New Holland, Ohio, has horns measuring more than 10 ft (3 m) from tip to tip.

R EXPENSIVE SHEEP

A young male Texel sheep—a breed highly prized for its lean meat—was sold at a Scottish livestock market for over $350,000 in 2009. The young ram, who could father up to 1,000 lambs per year, cost more than $1,500 per pound, which means that a lamb chop from it would cost about $600!

R RECYCLED PHONE

In 2009, a pelican at Tautphaus Park Zoo, Idaho, swallowed and later regurgitated a cell phone that a visitor had dropped into the pool.

R EARTHQUAKE PACKS

Pet owners in earthquake zones can buy special kits to ensure their cats and dogs survive. The Japanese-manufactured emergency packs contain a padded jacket and rain hat, special boots to protect paws, a bell in case the pet is lost in rubble, food, water and bowls, and aromatherapy oil to soothe stressed animals.

R TWO NOSES

A rabbit with two noses and four nostrils was discovered at a pet store in Milford, Connecticut, in 2009.

Inside Snout

In 2009, three piglets were born with their nostrils bizarrely inside the upper part of their lip. Half of a litter, born in the village of Jingdezhen, eastern China, had the rare deformity, but they still managed to eat, drink, and breathe normally despite having no snout.

℞ SUPER RAT

A new species of rat has been discovered in Papua New Guinea that is as big as a domestic cat! Found in the crater of the extinct volcano Mount Bosavi, the Bosavi woolly rat measures more than 32 in (80 cm) from nose to tail and weighs 3 lb (1.4 kg).

℞ ARROW SURGERY

A puppy from Kent, England, survived after swallowing a 10½-in (27-cm) plastic arrow that was almost as long as her. Betty, an eight-month-old Staffordshire bull terrier, underwent emergency surgery to remove the arrow, which had become lodged in her body from the esophagus to the small intestine.

22 POUNDS!

℞ ODD TWINS

When farmer Vic Phillips from Somerset, England, mated his Aberdeen Angus bull with a Simmental heifer, the latter gave birth to twins—of different breeds. The male calf is a Simmental, yet the female is an Aberdeen Angus.

℞ WANDERER RETURNS

A dog that vanished on the Gold Coast in Queensland, Australia, in 2000 was found nine years later and 1,250 mi (2,000 km) away in Melbourne, Victoria. While cleaning terrier-cross Muffy, animal carers spotted the microchip that identified her and enabled her to be reunited with her owners, the Lampard family.

℞ LUCKY BREAK

After chasing a rabbit over a 40-ft (12-m) cliff on the Isle of Wight, England, Mac the golden retriever escaped plunging to his death when his collar caught on some rocks, breaking his fall.

℞ CONTACT LENSES

A German company has invented a range of contact lenses for animals that suffer from cataracts, a condition that invariably leaves them blind. Among animals that may be able to be treated are lions, giraffes, bears, sea lions, kangaroos, and tigers.

Porky Puss

In 2009, the People's Dispensary for Sick Animals started a fat-fighting club for animals with weight problems, and Socrates the cat was one of nine chosen animals. The fat cat from Newcastle, England, loves to eat cheese-and-onion potato chips and weighs a massive 22 lb (10 kg). This is more than double his ideal weight and makes him "morbidly obese." The animals in the fitness club are put on a strict diet and exercise regime for 100 days to increase their life "pet-spectancy" and the most improved creature (and its owner) wins a vacation.

℞ MATERNAL INSTINCT

King penguins often adopt other penguins' chicks as their own and have been seen trying to raise a young skua—a species of bird that feeds on young penguins!

℞ NO JAWS

Horseshoe crabs have no jaws to chew with. Instead, they shove food straight into their open mouth with a pair of arms.

℞ FLOOD DIVERSION

During floods, Amazon River dolphins leave the river to swim through submerged forests lying in the flood plains.

℞ ETERNAL YOUTH

The fully grown, jellyfish-like creature *Turritopsis nutricula* can transform itself back into a juvenile an infinite number of times, keeping it from ever dying of old age.

℞ DUNG DWELLERS

Frogs in Sri Lanka's Bundala National Park have set up home in piles of Asian elephant dung. The frogs normally live among leaf litter on the ground, but because that can be in short supply during the dry season, they use elephant dung as an alternative habitat.

℞ UNINVITED GUEST

When Vickie Mendenhall from Spokane, Washington, bought a used couch for $27 in 2009, she found a cat living inside it. The cat had climbed in through a small hole on the underside when the couch's previous owner had donated it to the Value Village store.

℞ GREEN ENERGY

In 2008, the state of Michigan passed a new law that allows roadkill and other rotting animal carcasses to be converted into green energy. Bacteria and enzymes break down the carcasses and produce gas that can be used in engines and create electricity.

℞ SMOOTH SKIN

Elephants at Belfast Zoo in Northern Ireland have been given a brand of supermarket moisturizer to keep their bottoms smooth. Keeper Aisling McMahon recommended the moisturizing cream she used on her own skin and now the elephants receive regular applications to soften unwanted dry skin around their lower feet and butt.

℞ SLEEPY CEPHALOPOD

The Australian giant cuttlefish spends a remarkable 95 percent of its day resting and hiding in crevices from predators.

℞ SHARK SHOCK

A bamboo shark was born out of water in 2009 while being moved at an aquarium in Cheshire, England. The egg was being carefully transferred to a quarantine section at the Blue Planet Aquarium when it unexpectedly hatched in a diver's hands.

℞ TRAPPED UNDERGROUND

A Jack Russell terrier was trapped for 25 days underground in a rabbit warren in 2009—until he lost so much weight that he was able to crawl out. Six-year-old Jake was out walking with his owner Richard Thomas in Haverfordwest, Wales, when he chased a rabbit down a hole. When he failed to reappear, he was feared dead, but nearly a month later a new slimline Jake finally scrambled out, courtesy of his enforced diet.

℞ DOLPHIN TALK

In addition to using audible clicks and whistles, dolphins "talk" to each other by slapping their tail. Spanish scientists have observed that dolphins use various body movements, which also include diving and flopping sideways on the surface, as a means of communication.

Whale of a Tongue

When an unfortunate finback whale washed up dead on a beach in Provincetown, Massachusetts, in 2009, the gases that were given off during the decomposition process caused its tongue to swell up like a giant balloon. Finbacks are the second biggest creatures on Earth after the blue whale and this young specimen was 40 ft (12 m) long and weighed about 22,000 lb (10,000 kg).

RIPLEY'S RESEARCH

ALBINISM IS A GENETIC TRAIT CHARACTERIZED BY A LACK OF MELANIN IN THE BODY, WHICH RESULTS IN A LACK OF PIGMENT. THIS GIVES ALBINO ANIMALS, AND PEOPLE, THEIR DISTINCTIVE WHITE COLORING. IT IS HIGHLY UNUSUAL, HOWEVER, FOR AN ALBINO ANIMAL, SUCH AS THIS DOLPHIN, TO BE SO UNIFORMLY AND BRIGHTLY PINK IN COLOR. MANY ALBINO ANIMALS SUFFER IN THE SUN AS MELANIN PROTECTS AGAINST ULTRAVIOLET LIGHT, BUT APART FROM SPENDING A LITTLE MORE TIME UNDER THE SURFACE, "PINKY" IN CALCASIEU LAKE SHOWS NO SIGNS OF THIS.

Pink Dolphin

Never before seen, a bright pink albino bottlenose dolphin has been catching the eye of sailors on coastal Calcasieu Lake, Louisiana. The dolphin, which has grown up in the area, is perfectly healthy apart from its flawless pink finish. The young creature swims with a small pod of fellow dolphins in the lake and is an unforgettable attraction for those lucky enough to catch a glimpse.

℞ SWEET TOOTH

A bear with a sweet tooth broke into a San Bernardino County, California, home and ate a 2-lb (900-g) box of chocolates from the refrigerator. He pushed aside vegetables in the fridge and went straight for the chocolates. He also tried unsuccessfully to open a bottle of champagne.

℞ POODLE STANDS

A poodle in Xi'an City, China, goes for a walk every day—on two feet. Gou Gou draws large crowds by walking hand-in-paw with owner Wang Guoqiang who taught the dog to walk on its two back legs as a puppy.

℞ DEEP DIVE

Sperm whales can dive to depths of nearly 2 mi (3 km) and can stay underwater for up to 90 minutes at a time without needing to surface for breath.

℞ JUMPING SQUID

Some species of squid leap from the water and glide through the air to evade predators.

℞ SURFING DOG

An eight-month-old Border terrier can ride waves up to 3 ft (1 m) high near his home in Cornwall, England. Trained by owner Tim Kevan, Jack regularly surfs on a 9-ft (3-m) board and can even perform tricks such as a "hang five," where he walks up and down the board while surfing.

℞ FISH FANGS

Danionella dracula, a species of fish in Myanmar, has bone spurs that grow through the skin of its mouth and act as fangs.

℞ SWIMMING AID

A shark's skin is covered in tiny toothlike structures called denticles, which help it swim with a minimum of friction.

℞ FANTASTIC FINBACK

For many years Cambridge University in England has displayed the 70-ft (21-m) skeleton of a finback whale at its Zoology Museum. The specimen was found in 1865 on a beach in Sussex, England, and would have weighed 176,000 lb (80 tons).

Sea Pig

This curious creature was caught in deep water by the Cabrillo Marine Aquarium in California. It is about the size of an apple and can be found in most of the world's oceans at depths greater than 330 ft (100 m). It is actually a type of squid, and what looks like hair is really a crop of tentacles attached to its head. Orange pigments on its body can look like facial features when its body swells with water. Add to this a protruding noselike "siphon," which it uses to propel itself, and you have what is commonly known as the Piglet Squid.

Fly-vertising

At the 2009 Frankfurt Book Fair, a German publishing company started a new advertising craze, attaching very small banners to flies and letting them loose around the halls of the fair. Eichborn, whose logo is a fly, decided to attach the lightweight banners saying "The Publisher of the Fly" to 200 flies to promote their advertising stand. The banners were attached using string and wax that would fall off naturally without harming the fly. However, the flies did have some difficulty staying in the air and kept landing on people all over the convention.

EICHBORN der verlag mit der fliege · Halle 4 | Stand E146

Fortunate Feline

When Chase, a kitten from Lexington, Kentucky, was hit by a car she lost her nose, eyelids, and the skin on her face, as well as one of her legs. Surgeons were unable to rebuild her features, so she was left with pink tissue instead of fur on her face. She was adopted by Melissa Smith, the veterinary technician who had helped look after her, and has since become a "therapy cat" in the local area, helping people with disfigurements to improve their confidence. Chase has even become an online celebrity with her own blog that reassures her fans that she is happy and not in any pain.

℞ LUCKY FELIX

In April 2009, Felix, a 12-year-old cat belonging to Andrea Schröder of Cologne, Germany, was found alive despite having been trapped in the rubble of a collapsed apartment building for nearly five weeks.

℞ FOXY THIEF

Over several months, a fox in Germany stole more than 120 shoes from homes and gardens near Föhren. A forestry worker found the missing footwear in and around the fox's lair, the tiny tooth marks on the leather suggesting that the vixen may have used them as toys for her cubs to play with.

℞ DANCING COLLIE

Samson, a border collie dog from Manchester, England, loves disco dancing. He can perform twirls, spins, and jumps in time to his favorite music, and can even stand on his back legs to do his own version of Michael Jackson's moonwalk.

℞ TOILET PYTHON

Erik Rantzau found a python almost twice his size coiled up in the toilet bowl of his house near Darwin, Northern Territory, Australia. The 10-ft-long (3-m) carpet python had been seen roaming in the garden for years before deciding to set up home in his toilet.

℞ CAMEL IMPORTS

Camels aren't native to Australia, but the continent has about one million of them roaming its rural interior.

℞ FREAK EGG

Thelma, a chicken owned by Margaret Hamstra of Lynden, Washington State, laid an oversized egg—8 in (20 cm) in circumference—with a normal egg inside. Each egg had both a white and a yolk.

℞ PAINTING POOCH

Ziggy, a Pekingese dog owned by Elizabeth Monacelli of southern California, paints works of art that have sold for up to $250 at auctions. He creates his masterpieces by putting his teeth around a paper towel roll, which is attached to a paintbrush. Monacelli plays him special Chinese music to get him in the artistic mood, but even then he manages an average of only three brushstrokes per painting session before curling into a ball and falling asleep.

℞ ELEPHANT SLIPPERS

In a bid to soothe painful abscesses on her front feet, Gay, a 40-year-old Asian elephant at Paignton Zoo, Devon, England, has been fitted with a pair of $750 slippers. To ensure a good fit, keepers had to draw an outline around her two front feet to make patterns that were then sent off to a specialist firm in Australia. Each slipper boot measures about 16 in (40 cm) in diameter and comes with laces that elephants can't undo.

Purrfectly content!

MEAT FEAST

MANE MEAL
ENCOURAGING HUNGRY LIONS TO LEAP ONTO YOUR CAR MIGHT NOT SEEM VERY SMART, BUT THAT IS THE IDEA BEHIND A NEW EXHIBIT AT WERRIBEE OPEN RANGE ZOO IN VICTORIA, AUSTRALIA. ALTHOUGH IT LOOKS AS IF THERE IS NOTHING PROTECTING THE TOURISTS FROM BECOMING THIS LION'S NEXT MEAL, A CLOSER LOOK REVEALS A SHEET OF GLASS IN FRONT OF THE STEERING WHEEL, SO THAT PASSENGERS CAN GET CLOSE TO BIG CATS AS THEY FEED.

℞ FELINE PASSENGER
For over four years, a cat in Plymouth, England, has been catching the same bus every day. Casper boards the number 3 bus at 10.55 a.m. outside his home and travels the entire 11-mi (18-km) route before returning home an hour later. He is such a regular passenger that bus drivers look out for him to make sure he gets off at the right stop.

℞ FLUFFY FISH
A pet goldfish survived out of water for seven hours after apparently jumping out of his tank. Sparkle was found covered in dog hairs and fluff behind the tank's stand in North Yorkshire, England, but after being washed under the faucet, he started breathing again and made a full recovery.

℞ TEN-INCH TONGUE
The pangolin, a rare African animal, has a tongue that can extend up to 16 in (40 cm), which it uses to lap up termites and ants.

℞ DRUNKEN BADGER
German police were called to deal with a dead badger on the road near the town of Goslar—only to find that the animal was not dead at all, merely drunk! The badger had staggered into the middle of the road after eating overripe cherries that had fermented.

℞ SEA BUDGIE
A budgerigar that had escaped from its aviary in the coastal town of Brixham in Devon, England, was found floating half a mile out to sea. The bedraggled bird was plucked from the water by a dive-boat crew and reunited with its owner, budgie breeder Mike Peel.

℞ GOAT ARRESTED
A vigilante group in Kwara State, Nigeria, turned a goat over to police in January 2009, convinced that it was a car thief who had used black magic to change his form.

℞ GUCCI POOCHES
Dogs wearing designer outfits ranging from polka-dot bathing suits to glitzy evening wear took to the catwalk during a fashion show in Taipei, Taiwan, in July 2009.

℞ NON-SWIMMERS
Although adult hippos are well adapted to aquatic life—they can see underwater and hold their breath for several minutes—they can't swim or float. Their bodies are too dense to have any natural buoyancy, so they move around either by pushing off from the bottom of the river or by walking along the riverbed.

℞ CLEVER DOGS
Dogs may be as intelligent as two-year-old children. Animal psychologists at the University of British Columbia in Vancouver, Canada, have found that dogs are able to understand up to 250 "human" words and gestures, can count up to five, and can even perform simple mathematical calculations.

A Soaring Squeeze

Swallows travel at an amazing 35 mph (56 km/h), and when faced with an obstacle, such as a 2-in (5-cm) gap, they simply maneuver their 14-in (36-cm) wings and continue flying. The birds use their v-shaped tail to make sudden dramatic turns that enable them to squeeze through tiny gaps as well as snatch bugs out of the air.

℞ CORPSE CARPET

Thousands of generations of Bogong moths have been spending their summers in caves in the Australian Alps, their dead bodies forming a carpet 5 ft (1.5 m) deep.

℞ ADOPTED OWL

An orphaned baby eagle owl was adopted by a springer spaniel at a bird of prey rescue center in Cornwall, England, in 2009. The pair became inseparable and Sophie the spaniel even gave Bramble the owl a daily wash by licking her.

℞ GIANT WORM

The giant Gippsland earthworm, which lives in Victoria, Australia, can reach lengths of 10 ft (3 m). The young are already 8 in (20 cm) long when they hatch and take about five years to reach maturity. When the giant worm was first discovered in the 1870s, its size led scientists to think it was a snake.

℞ FATAL REPAIRS

Some aphids use goo from their body to patch holes in their colony's home—but often die in the process.

℞ PEPPERMINT SPRAY

Australia's peppermint stick insects spray an irritating, peppermint-scented fluid to defend themselves against predators.

℞ PIGEON SMUGGLERS

In March 2009, Brazilian police discovered inmates raising homing pigeons within Danilo Pinheiro Prison, Sorocaba, for the purpose of smuggling in contraband. Guards intercepted two pigeons carrying cell phones and chargers to detainees.

℞ STAR WITNESS

In April 2009, Judge James Martz of Palm Beach County, Florida, ordered a parrot to appear in court for a custody dispute involving the bird.

℞ DOG'S GUIDE DOG

A blind Border collie has his own guide dog! Five-year-old Clyde is totally blind and relies on another collie, Bonnie, to help him around the dog rescue center in Norfolk, England. Clyde refuses to go anywhere without Bonnie, who stays inches from his side while guiding him on walks or to food and water. She even lets him rest his head on her haunches when he becomes disorientated.

℞ DANCING CATERPILLARS

Birch sawfly larvae do a group dance routine to put off predators while they are munching through leaves. As many as six caterpillars will rear up with their back legs simultaneously to make themselves look more imposing.

℞ GIANT RABBIT

Benny, a two-year-old giant Flemish buck rabbit owned by Martin and Sharon Heather of Oxfordshire, England, is nearly 3 ft (90 cm) long and tips the scales at over 22 lb (10 kg). His food bill tops $75 a week.

ACTUAL SIZE!

A LITTLE PREY-ER

These other tiny animals also have bizarre ways of protecting themselves.

● **The Pebble Toad**, which lives on the top of the Venezuelan mountains, has a magnificent method of defense when facing danger. It curls up into a ball, tenses its body, and rolls down the side of a mountain, bouncing like a falling pebble.

● **The River Frog** has a bizarre way of defending itself against predators. Instead of running from danger, it will turn over and play dead—its body goes completely limp. Predators would much prefer live food and so leave the "dead" frog alone.

● **The Goldenrod Spider** is able to change colors, like a chameleon, by secreting a yellow liquid onto its body. This is particularly useful for hiding from its predators, and prey, in bright flowers.

● **The Hagfish** is one of the smallest fish in the ocean. When it is in danger, it releases huge amounts of mucus all over its body to make itself slippery. The predator cannot get hold of the fish and suffocates.

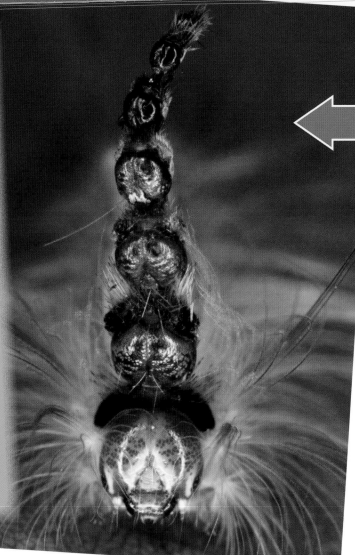

Mad Hatterpillar

This gum leaf skeletoniser caterpillar, commonly known in Australia as a hatterpillar, cleverly defends itself by stacking up its past head cases like hats on top of its head. Found all over New Zealand and Australia, the hatterpillar molts heads as it grows larger and during this process grows a spike on the top its head. Retaining each head case that falls off, the hatterpillar is able to stick each one onto the spike, sometimes having as many as six heads (or hats!) on top.

Ⓡ FIERCE FROG

A species of frog that lived in Madagascar some 70 million years ago was so big and aggressive that it may even have eaten baby dinosaurs. Larger than any frog living today, *Beelzebufo ampinga* was 16 in (40 cm) long, weighed around 10 lb (4.5 kg) and possessed a very wide mouth and powerful jaws.

Ⓡ CLOSE CALL

A tiny Chihuahua, weighing about 4 lb (1.8 kg), somehow survived and recovered after being trodden on by her best friend— a 1,980-lb (900-kg) Clydesdale horse. Little Berry was playing with her friend Leroy at their home in Geelong, Victoria, Australia, when the giant horse accidentally stepped on the dog's head.

SNAIL TRAIL

THE GIANT AFRICAN SNAIL IS ONE OF THE WORLD'S MOST DESTRUCTIVE CREATURES AND CAN GROW UP TO 10 IN (25 CM) IN LENGTH. FOUND MOSTLY IN EAST AFRICA, ASIA, AND THE CARIBBEAN, THEY GO GLOBAL BY CLIMBING INTO PRODUCE CONTAINERS AND SAILING ALL OVER THE WORLD. IN 1966, A BOY FROM MIAMI, FLORIDA, ACQUIRED THREE OF THESE SNAILS, WHICH HIS GRANDMA RELEASED INTO A GARDEN. SEVEN YEARS LATER, THERE WERE 18,000 OF THEM AND IT TOOK THE FLORIDA AUTHORITIES TEN YEARS AND $1 MILLION TO ERADICATE THEM.

Ⓡ FAITHFUL FRIEND

Buddy, a German Shepherd dog, has phoned for help on three separate occasions when his owner, Joe Stalnaker of Scottsdale, Arizona, was incapacitated by seizures. Amazingly, the emergency operators took the calls from the clever hound to save its owner's life.

Ⓡ LONG BUG

Chan's megastick, a stick-insect bug discovered on the island of Borneo by a Malaysian naturalist in 1989, measures 22 in (55 cm) long! Its body alone, without the legs, measures a staggering 14 in (35 cm).

Ⓡ INSECT COLLECTION

Founded as part of the British Museum in 1756, London's Natural History Museum has nearly nine million butterflies and moths in its collection.

Ⓡ SPINY NEWT

The Iberian ribbed newt, found in Morocco, Portugal, and Spain, has sharply pointed ribs that it can stick through its sides to protect against predators.

℞ SHARK JUMP

In December 2008, a reef shark at a Bahamas resort jumped from its aquarium, landed on a nearby water slide, slid down to the swimming pool, and surprised the staff.

℞ JUNK FOOD

Zeke, a cat owned by the Scarpino family of Cedar Knolls, New Jersey, had surgery to remove more than a year's accumulation of hair ties, ribbon, twist ties, and junk from his stomach—which had grown to five times its normal size.

℞ CANINE CASTAWAY

A pet dog that was swept overboard on a sailing trip swam 5 mi (8 km) through shark-infested waters and survived on a remote island for four months by feeding on baby goats. The grey and black cattle dog was reunited with owners Jan and Dave Griffith after being found by rangers on the largely uninhabited St. Bees Island off the coast of Queensland, Australia.

℞ PUSHY PORKER

A pig the size of a Shetland pony terrorized a woman in Murwillumbah, New South Wales, Australia, in 2008. The pig took up residence at the home of Caroline Hayes and refused to leave her alone.

℞ HOPPING MAD

A kangaroo burst through the window of a house and hopped into bed with a startled Australian family in March 2009. Beat Ettlin rescued his children from the kangaroo that stood around 6 ft (1.8 m) tall by wrestling the animal into a headlock and dragging it down the hall and out the front door.

℞ ESCAPE BID

An ingenious orangutan tried to escape from an Australian zoo in May 2009 by short-circuiting an electric fence. Twenty-seven-year-old Karta jammed a stick into wires connected to the fence and then piled up sufficient debris to enable her to scale a concrete and glass wall at Adelaide Zoo. On reaching the top of the fence, she sat there for 30 minutes before changing her mind and returning to the enclosure.

℞ COLOMBIAN MONSTER

An extinct species of snake, which lived in Colombian jungles 58 million years ago, could reach lengths of up to 42 ft (13 m)—that's longer than a bus.

℞ CRANE PURSUIT

Conservationists in Wisconsin help endangered whooping cranes to migrate south for the winter by encouraging them to fly in pursuit of a microlight plane. The hand-reared birds are taught that the microlight, which plays recordings of simulated crane calls, is their parent, so when the aircraft takes off, they dutifully follow for more than 1,250 mi (2,000 km) to the warmth and safety of the west coast of Florida.

℞ CLONED PET

A Florida family paid $155,000 for a clone of their dead dog. Nina Otto from Boca Raton had the DNA of her beloved golden Labrador, Sir Lancelot, collected and frozen five years before his death in 2008. In 2009, the family collected Lancelot Encore, a three-month-old puppy that was an exact genetic replica of their deceased pet.

℞ BOUNCING FISH

A new species of fish has been discovered that bounces on the ocean floor like a rubber ball. The psychedelic dogfish, which was discovered off the coast of Indonesia in 2008, bounces around in a haphazard manner because its tail is off-center and because it propels itself forward jerkily by expelling water from tiny gill openings.

BAY OF PIGS

SWIMMERS OFF THE BIG MAJOR SPOT ISLAND IN THE BAHAMAS ARE AMAZED TO SEE FERAL PIGS ENJOYING THE CRYSTAL CLEAR WATER. THE AREA IS KNOWN LOCALLY AS "PIG BEACH," AND NOBODY IS QUITE SURE HOW THE PIGS GOT THERE. THE ISLAND IS UNINHABITED EXCEPT FOR VISITORS BRINGING SCRAPS FOR THE GROWING PIG POPULATION, WHO PADDLE OUT TO BOATS TO MAKE SURE THEY GET THE FOOD FIRST.

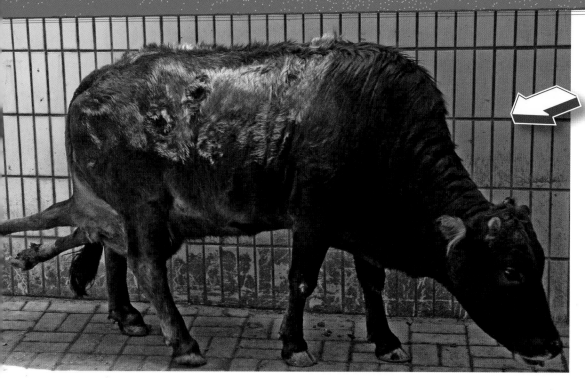

Cow Strange

This six-year-old cow was born with six legs and can be seen in a zoo in Yichang, China. Unsurprisingly, it is a big hit with the visitors. The condition, known as "Polymelia," can affect most animals, and may be caused by a genetic disorder, a deformed twin being partially absorbed in the womb, or environmental issues.

℞ BLOWN AWAY

A Chihuahua swept up into the air and blown away by a 70-mph (110-km/h) gust of wind was eventually found safe and sound more than a mile (1.6 km) away. Weighing 6 lb (2.7 kg), little eight-month-old Tinker Bell was standing on her owners' platform trailer at a flea market in Waterford Township, Michigan, in April 2009 when she was hurled out of sight by the force of the sudden blast of air.

℞ MAGNETIC CROCS

Biologists in Florida tape magnets to the heads of nuisance crocodiles to disrupt their magnetic sense of direction when they relocate the animals.

℞ TV ADDICT

A pet rabbit in Xiamen, China, is so addicted to South Korean TV soap operas that she attacks her owners if they change the channel while she is watching. Every night at 10 p.m., the rabbit, Jia Xiaoyu, climbs between the couple to watch an imported drama, but starts biting the pillow and becoming aggressive if her favorite show, *Ms. Mermaid*, isn't on.

℞ SNAKE BITE

Johannes Swart spent 37 days in a glass box, measuring 16 x 13 ft (5 x 4 m), with 40 highly venomous snakes at a conservation park near Pretoria, South Africa, in September 2009. His stay ended when he was bitten on the foot by a deadly puff adder and had to undergo emergency surgery in the local hospital.

℞ WHISTLING APES

An orangutan at the National Zoo in Washington, D.C. has amazed keepers by learning to whistle. Thirty-two-year-old Bonnie taught herself after listening to keepers whistling while they worked. She is thought to have taught another orangutan at the zoo to whistle, too.

℞ MAN BITES SNAKE

A Kenyan man escaped from a python by biting it after the snake had wrapped him in its coils and dragged him up a tree. During the three-hour struggle, Ben Nyaumbe smothered the snake's head with his shirt to prevent it from swallowing him and then bit the python on the tip of its tail.

Snake Boy

Uorn Sambath from Setbo, Cambodia, has an unusual pet for a boy. He has developed a friendship with a huge 16-ft (4.9-m) python. He gives the serpent hugs and kisses and sometimes sleeps inside the coils of the snake, which weighs over 220 lb (100 kg) and requires three adults to carry it. The python first slithered into the boy's bedroom when he was three months old, and now has its own room in the family home.

Mad MENaGERie

VENICE BEACH FREAKSHOW

VENICE BEACH FREAKSHOW

RIPLEY'S ask

Why did you create the Freakshow?
I have been a collector of circus, sideshow, and Freakshow memorabilia since I was a kid. I started the Freakshow to show kids of all ages the wonders of the universe, to remind them that life is a special gift in all of its amazing forms. When I was a kid, I visited a similar show and was never the same. I loved it! There is nothing in the world like the look of wonder in a kid's eyes when they see a living two-headed animal. It's as though the entire world is new to them. That is why I created the Venice Beach Freakshow, to raise those questions on the mysteries of life and to celebrate the magnificence and majesty of creation with children of all ages.

Todd holding Myrtle and Squirtle, who share the same shell, outside his Venice Beach Freakshow

TODD RAY'S "FREAKSHOW" HOUSES ONE OF THE STRANGEST COLLECTIONS OF LIVE CREATURES ON THE PLANET. TODD ESTABLISHED HIS MENAGERIE OF ANIMALS ON THE BEACH BOARDWALK AT VENICE, CALIFORNIA, AFTER RETIRING FROM A CAREER IN THE MUSIC INDUSTRY. HIS COLLECTION CONTAINS TURTLES, SNAKES, AND LIZARDS WITH MULTIPLE HEADS, A DOG WITH FIVE LEGS, AN IGUANA WITH TWO TAILS, A HAIRLESS RAT, ALBINO SNAKES, AND MANY OTHER ODDITIES. INSIDE THE SHOW ARE LESS FORTUNATE FREAKS OF THE NATURAL WORLD, SUCH AS DOUBLE-HEADED COWS, CHICKENS, AND EVEN A RACCOON, PRESERVED IN JARS OF FORMALDEHYDE FOR CURIOUS VISITORS TO SEE.

One of the many oddities in Todd's extended collection, a two-faced kitten preserved in formaldehyde

Double-tailed iguana

Cheech and Chong, a turtle with two heads and six legs

Double-headed bearded dragon

Rocky the five-legged miniature pinscher, held by Todd's daughter Asia

Laverne and Shirley the two-headed kingsnake

Giant Limb

Motola, a 48-year-old Asian elephant from Thailand, needed a heavyweight solution when she lost part of one of her legs after stepping on a land mine ten years ago. After trying various prototypes, she was recently fitted with a custom-made permanent prosthetic limb strong enough to hold her weight at the Elephant Hospital in North Thailand. The jumbo operation to fit Motola's new leg required enough anesthetic to knock out 70 people.

℞ DOLPHIN RESCUE

In April 2009, thousands of leaping dolphins in the Gulf of Aden prevented Somali pirate speedboats from attacking a flotilla of Chinese merchant ships. When the dolphins, which were swimming next to the Chinese ships, leaped out of the water, the pirates decided to turn back.

℞ SPORTING PENGUINS

In May 2009, New Zealand hosted the world's first sports tournament for penguins. The Penguathlon took place in Orakei, near Auckland, and saw king and gentoo penguins go beak to beak in five events— football, Frisbee, surfing, swing ball, and waddle racing.

℞ ZEBRA RIDE

Former racehorse jockey Bill Turner rides a zebra to his local pub in the town of Sherborne in Dorset, England. He bought the zebra from a game reserve in Holland and learned to ride it in just two weeks.

℞ OCTOPUS STUDY

British marine experts have discovered that instead of eight arms, an octopus really has only six. A new study has revealed that it uses six of its tentacles as arms for eating, but the back two limbs act as legs to help it move across the ocean floor.

℞ METAL CROC

Doug Mader, a veterinarian in Marathon, Florida, used four metal rods and 41 screws to reconstruct the jaw of a crocodile that had its head crushed by a car in December 2008.

℞ DENTAL CARE

Female long-tailed macaque monkeys near Bangkok, Thailand, have been observed teaching their young how to floss their teeth. The adults were seen using strands of hair to clean between their teeth, and this practice became more regular and more elaborate when the females were with their babies, suggesting that they were trying to teach the youngsters the importance of good dental hygiene.

℞ 15,000 FEET

The sunflower starfish grows to a diameter of more than 3 ft (1 m) across and has around 15,000 tube feet on the underside of its body.

Crocodile Man

Chito Loco thinks nothing of frolicking in the water with a 980-lb (445-kg) crocodile. Chito rescued the giant reptile after farmers shot him 20 years ago, and nursed him back to health. The Costa Rican fisherman now puts on a weekly show during which he feeds and even rides the croc, which he named Pocho, who is an impressive 16 ft (5 m) long.

MEAT EATER

INTREPID EXPLORERS HAVE RELEASED DETAILS OF AN AMAZING NEW PLANT SPECIES, CAPABLE OF TRAPPING AND DEVOURING A FULL-SIZE RAT, ON AN ISLAND IN THE PHILIPPINES. IN A QUEST TO FIND THE PLANT, WHICH WAS LAST RECORDED IN 1907, STEWART MCPHERSON'S TEAM CLIMBED A MOUNTAIN IN THE MIDDLE OF A PRISON, GUIDED BY THREE CONVICTED MURDERERS, AND DISCOVERED THE CARNIVOROUS PITCHER PLANTS AT THE SUMMIT. THE PLANTS ARE THE SIZE OF FOOTBALLS AND LINED WITH TENTACLES THAT SECRETE STICKY GLUE TO ENSNARE INSECTS AND RODENTS, BEFORE IT DISSOLVES THEM WITH ITS ACID-LIKE ENZYMES.

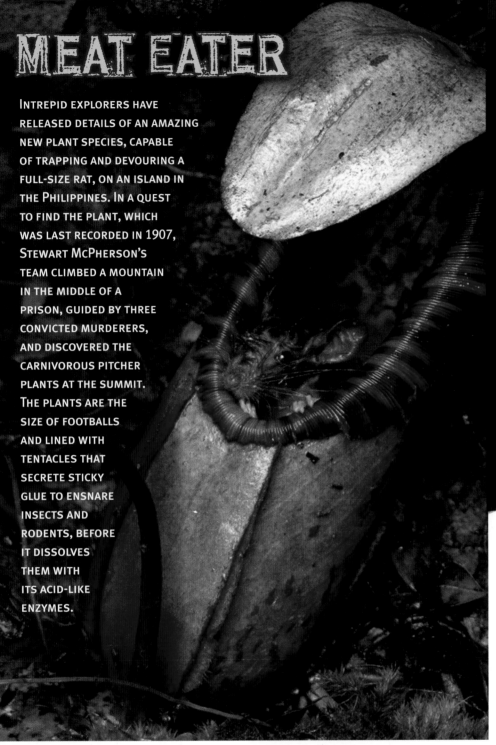

Weird Vegetation

Dragon Arum At night the flowers of this plant trap flies attracted by its smell of rotting meat. The plant lets them go free in the morning so they can transfer its pollen.

Mimosa pudica Its name means "shy plant," and if it is touched or exposed to heat its branches shrink away and its leaves curl up.

Hydnora africana This is a parasitic plant with a feces-like odor that attracts dung beetles who then help to pollinate the plant.

Titan Arum One of the largest flowers in the world, it smells like dead animals and only flowers once every six or seven years.

Common Bladderwort This is an aquatic plant capable of trapping and digesting worms, tadpoles, and even young fish.

℞ HOT HIPPO

A hippopotamus that decided to escape the South African heat by climbing into a 10-ft-high (3-m) water tower for a long soak found it couldn't get out again. A farm worker realized the animal was stuck, and in a four-hour operation a team from the Mpumalanga Tourism and Parks Association drained the tank and used poles to nudge the hippo into a steel cage before winching it to safety with a hydraulic crane.

℞ PANDA-MONIUM

In June 2009, keepers at Thailand's Ayutthaya Elephant Kraal painted five of their elephants in black and white watercolor paint to make them look like giant pandas! The bizarre move was intended to raise the profile of the elephant—Thailand's national symbol—after the whole country had gone panda-crazy since the birth of a female panda cub at a zoo in Bangkok.

℞ SURPRISE VISITOR

In March 2009, a sick turtle swam directly to the Turtle Hospital—a turtle treatment facility in the Florida Keys! The 73-lb (33-kg) loggerhead turtle was found to be suffering from a bacterial infection.

℞ RAT PACK

White laboratory rats protect official police records in the city of Karnal in the Indian state of Haryana by scaring away mice that would damage paperwork and eat evidence.

℞ BEE SWARM

Employees at a game store in one of the busiest shopping areas of New York City were trapped inside for several hours in May 2009 while thousands of bees swarmed outside in the street. After a passerby managed to lure some of the bees into a box, a specialist arrived in protective gear and used the scent of a queen bee to collect the rest of them.

℞ FROZEN BUG

The Alpine weta of New Zealand, a large, cricket-like insect, can freeze solid for several months without suffering any ill effects.

℞ SEA HUNT

A fugitive sea lion tried to escape from Californian police officers in June 2009 by taking control of their speedboat. The animal, nicknamed Snoopy, was picked up by Orange County sheriffs after reports that he had bitten a boy in Newport Harbor. But once on board the patrol boat, the resourceful sea lion apparently managed to start the throttle, steer the boat, and even sound the siren.

Snake Foot

This snake was discovered in China in 2009 with a single clawed foot growing out from its body. The 16-in-long (40-cm) mutant reptile was found by Duan Qiongxiu clinging to the wall of her bedroom in Suining with its talons. Mrs. Duan was so scared that she beat the snake to death with her shoe. Growing a foot is a very rare mutation for a snake—they more frequently grow two heads—and scientists are working to find out if the foot evolved from changes in the snake's environment.

℞ CRUEL TWIST

A dog in China became so attached to two red pandas she had adopted that she rejected her own puppy. The rare pandas were abandoned by their mother shortly after being born at Taiyuan Zoo, but were nursed back to health with love and milk from the dog. However, the dog became convinced that the cubs were its own babies and refused to nurse her own puppy.

℞ SIGN LANGUAGE

A Border collie puppy is learning sign language after it was discovered that she is totally deaf. Pixie is being taught to recognize hand commands by trainer Liz Grewal in Coffs Harbour, New South Wales, Australia.

℞ PRESIDENT'S BEARS

U.S. President Thomas Jefferson received a gift of two grizzly bears in October 1807. He was so delighted that he kept them on the White House lawn for months.

℞ TOILET ORDEAL

A puppy survived being flushed down a lavatory in June 2009 after his four-year-old owner decided that his pet needed a wash. The week-old cocker spaniel was muddy following a walk, so young Daniel Blair of Middlesex, England, decided to wash it by putting it in the toilet and flushing it. The puppy was rescued by plumbers after being trapped in a waste pipe for nearly four hours.

℞ SILK BELL

Europe's water spider spends its entire life underwater and builds a silk diving bell to store oxygen.

℞ BEST FRIENDS

Gerald, a 15-ft-tall (4.5-m) giraffe at Noah's Ark Zoo Farm in Bristol, England, has an unusual best friend—a goat named Eddie. The pair have been inseparable for more than three years, with Gerald letting his little friend climb on his neck and share his bedding. He even chases away the zebras who bully Eddie.

℞ CATERPILLAR INVASION

The President of Liberia declared a state of emergency in January 2009 because of giant armies of caterpillars. In the worst invasion in 30 years, tens of millions of marching caterpillars swarmed over 80 towns and villages, preventing farmers from reaching their fields and causing others to flee their homes.

℞ CYANIDE GLANDS

The dragon millipede of Thailand has bright pink coloration and glands that produce cyanide poison.

℞ WEDDING GUEST

A dog who saved a woman's life after it found her dying of hypothermia was invited to be guest of honor at her wedding five years later. Zoe Christie had been discovered in November 2004 with severe hypothermia in a field in Devon, England, by John Richards and his boxer dog Boris. Mr. Richards had walked past Zoe's body, but Boris saw her and made such a commotion that his owner turned around and went back to see what the problem was.

℞ HOUSE GUESTS

Lesley Coles of Somerset, England, wondered why her shopping bag was heavy—and when she looked inside she found a 3-ft (90-cm) python curled up in the bottom. The snake was thought to have been secretly living in the cupboard of Mrs. Coles' house for up to six months after crawling in through a hole made for the electrical meter.

℞ GOOD MEMORY

Elephants can recognize groups of people by their specific smell, color, and the style of their clothing.

Incy Wincy Spider

The tiny "happy-face" spider can be found in the rainforests of only four islands in the world—Oahu, Molokai, Maui, and Hawaii. Measuring around 1/5 in (5 mm), no one really knows why the colorful patterns on the spiders' backs look like happy faces. One theory is that the patterns evolved to confuse their predators—birds—but the species is nevertheless under threat from a growing number of animals that have been introduced to the islands. Perhaps they need to evolve a scary face!

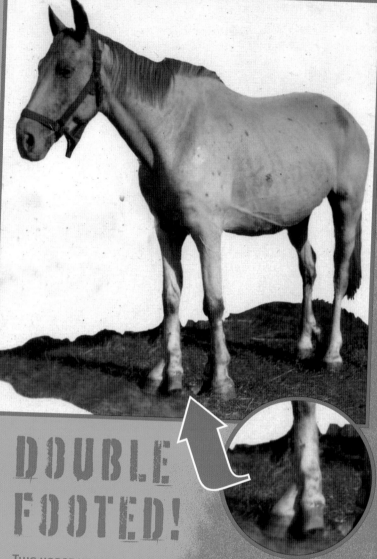

DOUBLE FOOTED!

THIS HORSE HAS TWO FEET! THE DOUBLE-FOOTED HORSE BELONGS TO R. VAN WERT OF CINCINNATI, OHIO, AND WAS PHOTOGRAPHED IN 1930. YOU WOULDN'T WANT THAT HOOF STANDING ON YOUR FOOT.

Clever Cat

Begging is a standard dog trick, but cats are intelligent animals so there is no reason why they cannot learn commands and tricks, as this photo proves. It was taken in 1930 and shows Red Gillette, from Tracy, California, feeding his pet cat from a spoon.

Living Dangerously

This performer at Barnum & Bailey Circus is demonstrating a bond of trust by placing himself inside an elephant's mouth. If there was any pressure from the creature's jaws it could crush the man's skull.

℞ TUNEFUL TOADS

In 2009, fire-bellied toads from Denmark, Germany, Latvia, and Sweden croaked it out for the second annual international toad song contest, held in the Schleswig-Holstein area of Germany.

℞ BOXER DOG

Chela, a dog owned by Peru's national police force, has been taught to box. Trainer Cesar Chacaliaza says the German shorthaired pointer wasn't keen on wearing boxing gloves at first, but she has now learned to jab with her front paws while standing up on her hind legs.

℞ TALENTED PIG

Sue, a kunekune pig owned by Wendy Scudamore from Herefordshire, England, shakes hands by presenting a trotter on command and can perform agility tests as ably as any dog. In fact, Mrs. Scudamore hopes that one day Sue will be able to herd sheep just like the pig in the movie *Babe*.

℞ LONG REACH

The Giant Pacific octopus has an arm span of more than 14 ft (4 m) across—that's greater than the height of two adult men.

℞ RUBBERY SKELETONS

Sharks, skates, and rays have skeletons made of cartilage—the same rubbery substance that gives shape to your ears and the bridge of your nose.

℞ FLYING CHIMP

Bili, a three-month-old bonobo chimpanzee, sat in the cabin with the rest of the passengers for his flight from Birmingham, England, to his new home at Frankfurt Zoo in Germany.

℞ WEASEL'S REVENGE

In 2009, Mr. Zhang of Wuchang, Hubei Province, China, said his family were being harassed by a weasel after he had caught its mate in a trap. Zhang said the male weasel excreted on tables, threw dead mice into the family home, and even jumped screaming onto their bed.

℞ SWALLOWED RING

Anne Moon from Yorkshire, England, lost a $2,250 antique diamond engagement ring in August 2009 when it was swallowed by a piglet. She went to pat Ginger, a ten-week-old kunekune pig, at a farm but it clamped its teeth around the ring and refused to let go.

℞ FATHER AT 110

In 2009, a tortoise living in Norfolk, England, became a father at age 110. Billy, a spur thigh tortoise, started a family after finally mating with Tammy, a 47-year-old female, who had rejected his advances for 15 years.

℞ ROVING EYE

The flounder is a fish with a migrating eye. At first the fish swim vertically with an eye on each side, but later one eye moves around to join the other and the fish start to swim flat.

℞ FREAKY PIG

A piglet born in Zhejiang Province, China, in 2009 had two mouths and three eyes. The mother was completely normal, as were the other seven piglets in the litter.

℞ CANINE COMMUTERS

Stray dogs in Moscow, Russia, use the subway to travel to the city center in search of food. They board the trains each morning and travel back on the subway to where they live in the evening. If they fall asleep and miss their stop, they get off and take another train back to the center.

Albino Turtle

RESEMBLING AN UNCOOKED CHRISTMAS TURKEY, THIS WHITE BEAST IS IN FACT A RARE ALBINO TURTLE. FOUND ON THE BANKS OF THE YELLOW RIVER IN HENAN PROVINCE, CHINA, IN 2009, IT MEASURES 16 IN (40 CM) IN LENGTH AND WEIGHS 14 LB (6.5 KG). THE MUTANT TURTLE REPORTEDLY ACQUIRED ITS ALL-WHITE SKIN, APART FROM ONE PINK PATCH, THROUGH A GENETIC MUTATION CAUSED BY POLLUTION.

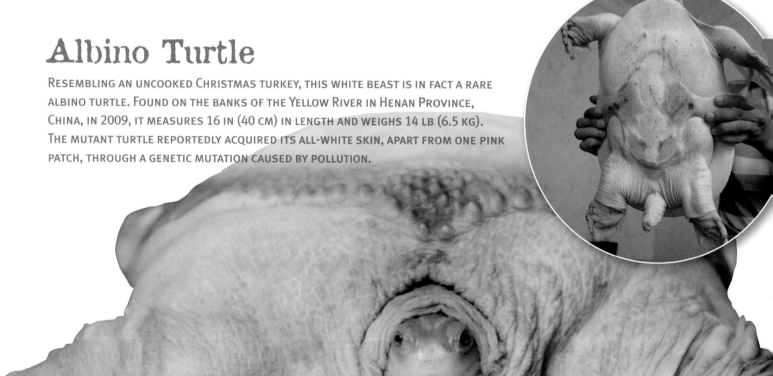

One Pig Race

Cushendun Community Fête, in Northern Ireland, enjoyed a fun-filled pig-racing event complete with colorful woolen jockeys in July 2009. Popular in the United States, the races are often a main attraction at county fairs. Only juvenile pigs are allowed to participate and they race around a grass or dirt track and even jump over hurdles.

℞ THREATENING KISS

In a bid to ward off predators, and to suggest that they are larger than they really are, orangutans make their voices sound deeper by blowing exaggerated kisses. They achieve the sound—called a kiss-squeak—by holding leaves or their hands up to their mouth.

℞ TURTLE RECALL

A runway at John F. Kennedy International Airport in New York City was shut down briefly in July 2009 after about 80 turtles emerged from nearby Jamaica Bay and crawled onto the tarmac. The invasion by the 8-in-long (20-cm) diamondback terrapins caused flights to be delayed for up to 90 minutes.

℞ DOG'S DINNER

When their dog Bertie started walking strangely, Mark and Michelle Jewell from Essex, England, took him to a veterinarian who found that nine golf balls were lodged in Bertie's stomach.

℞ LITERATE DOG

New York animal trainer Lyssa Rosenberg has taught her terrier Willow to read! Willow plays dead when she sees the word "bang," stretches a paw in the air when she sees "wave," and stands on her back feet to beg when she sees the words "sit up." Willow can do 250 different tricks and it took her just six weeks to recognize words and respond to them.

℞ AGED TORTOISE

Jonathan, a tortoise living on St. Helena Island, is estimated to be over 176 years old. The earliest photo of him, standing beside a Boer War prisoner, dates back more than 100 years.

℞ DACHSHUND DASH

San Diego, California, is home to the Wienerschnitzel Wiener Nationals—a sprint race created especially for dachshunds.

℞ SHARK SOUL

To put a male shark in the mood for love, staff at the Sea Life London Aquarium, England, piped the sounds of Barry White and Marvin Gaye into his tank. They hoped that the romantic music would encourage Zorro, a six-year-old zebra shark, to breed with a female, Mazawabee, who had been single for several years.

Monkey Business

Visitors at Knowsley Safari Park, Prescot, England, will need to learn to keep their luggage inside their cars after more than 20 resident baboons completely emptied visitors' suitcases in July 2009. The naughty baboons have cleverly worked out how to break into car roof racks leaving visitors no choice but to helplessly watch their belongings being strewn all over the ground! The incident has occurred so frequently that the Park's General Manager, David Ross, has had to advise cars with cargo cases not to drive through the monkey enclosure.

℞ TRACKING DEVICE

A 6-ft (1.8-m) python that was stolen from a research center near Perth, Western Australia, was traced by its last meal. The snake was snatched shortly after it had eaten a woylie, an endangered marsupial that, unbeknown to the unlucky thieves, had been fitted with a tracking device. The device showed up even from inside the python's stomach, alerting scientists and police to the snake's whereabouts.

℞ FROG FIND

Half a century after last being spotted, a population of rare California mountain yellow-legged frogs was rediscovered in 2009. The elusive amphibians were located in the San Bernardino National Forest by scientists following the same course as a 1908 expedition.

℞ ELEPHANT HANGED

On September 13, 1916, "Murderous Mary," an elephant from Sparks Brothers Circus, was hanged for killing a handler in Erwin, Tennessee. A crowd of 2,500 gathered to watch as the five-ton elephant was hanged by the neck by a chain attached to a 100-ton derrick car.

Short Legs

Fire crews were called out four times to rescue Mayflower, a gray Shetland pony apparently stuck in mud, only to find that the animal simply had short legs! Her unusually short legs and long body mean she is only half the height of other ponies grazing on salt marshes near the River Test in Hampshire, England.

℞ SENIOR DOG

Max, a terrier-cross belonging to Janelle Derouen of New Iberia, Louisiana, celebrated his 26th birthday in 2009—making him a staggering 182 years old in dog years.

℞ FIVE LEGS

Lilly, a Chihuahua puppy, was born in Gastonia, North Carolina, with five legs. The extra leg, which had no feeling, hung down between her two rear legs until it was removed at age seven weeks.

℞ DEEP DOWN

The Hadal snailfish lives at depths of 4.8 mi (7.7 km) under the Pacific Ocean in the Japan Trench, the deepest a fish has ever been filmed.

℞ COOKIE BEAR

A black bear was found sitting on a freezer eating cookies after breaking into a bakery in Tobermory, Ontario, Canada, in July 2009.

℞ TWISTED FLIGHT

When some geese come in to land from a great height, they fly upside down while keeping their head and neck the right way up! The display of contortionism, known as whiffling, enables the birds to release air from their wings and thus reduce their speed prior to landing.

℞ LUCKY STRIKE

A chicken in England has laid an egg shaped like a bowling pin! Natalie Wiltshire said the odd egg was laid by one of the 20 chickens she keeps in Willoughby, Northamptonshire.

℞ SHRINKING SHEEP

A breed of wild sheep in Scotland is shrinking in body size as a result of climate change. Since 1985, Soay sheep on the uninhabited island of Hirta in the St. Kilda archipelago have shrunk by five percent, their legs getting shorter and their body weight decreasing. In the past, only big sheep could survive the harsh winters in the area, but scientists say that because of climate change the winters have become milder and grass is now available for more months of the year, enabling smaller sheep to cope.

Mistaken Identity

Reggie, a 3-ft-long (1-m) kingsnake kept as a pet in West Sussex, England, required emergency surgery after attempting to eat his own tail. He mistook his tail for another snake but was unable to regurgitate it because of his backward-facing teeth. He was prevented from choking to death by veterinary surgeon Bob Reynolds, who pried open the snake's mouth, dislocated its jaw and removed the tail before it had been digested.

℞ TWO HEADS

A cobra with two heads was born in China in 2009. The cobra, which was able to eat by using both of its mouths simultaneously, hatched at the Jiujiang home of rail worker Mr. Liu, who breeds snakes as a hobby.

℞ PAMPERED PET

An Israeli woman paid $32,000 so that her boxer dog Orchuk could travel in business class with her from Paris, France, to Tel Aviv. She paid for an entire compartment to carry her, the dog, and a veterinarian on the four-hour El Al flight. The Israeli airline had to remove several seats to make way for the dog's cage.

℞ HORSE DRESS

Bavarian designer Hildegard Bergbauer usually creates traditional *dirndl* dresses for women, but now she has branched out and started making them for cats, dogs, and even horses, too!

℞ BEAR WITNESS

When naturalist Casey Anderson married actress Missi Pyle in Montana in 2009, his best man was Brutus, a half-ton grizzly bear. Brutus also joined the 85 guests at the reception, where he helped himself to some wedding cake. Having hand-reared the bear from a cub, Casey has forged a close relationship with the 7-ft-8-in-tall (2.3-m) animal. They walk and swim together and Casey has started teaching Brutus to fish.

℞ LIQUID LUNCH

Spiders are unable to eat solid food, so they must liquefy the insides of their prey. They do this by regurgitating digestive juices onto the prey and then crushing it with their jaws and sucking up the juices.

℞ BUTTERFLY HAVEN

There are almost 20,000 known species of butterflies and an amazing 40 percent of these are found in South America.

℞ NUCLEAR HOME

Half of the world's wild two-humped Bactrian camels live in a former nuclear weapons test site in Xinjiang, China.

℞ LOVE DARTS

About one-third of snail species grow "love darts," which they use when mating. The snails shoot the mucus-covered dart, which enhances fertility, into another snail's skin.

℞ BALD CAT

A cat who is bald apart from a mass of chest hair has become a tourist attraction at the Exeter Veterinary Hospital in New Hampshire because of his weird appearance. Eight-year-old Ugly Bat Boy, whose breed is not known, was adopted by Dr. Stephen Bassett shortly after he was born bald, probably as a result of a genetic defect.

℞ SWINGING DOG

Sara, a Labrador-chow cross, loves spending her days on the swings at her local park. She enjoys it so much that her owners, the Lanier family from Boone, North Carolina, take her to the park several times a week.

Cat Nap

BIG-CAT KEEPER RIANA VAN NIEUWENHUIZEN FROM BLOEMFONTEIN, SOUTH AFRICA, SHARES HER HOME WITH NINE CHEETAHS, THREE LEOPARDS, TWO WOLVES, A JAGUAR, A LION, AND THREE DOGS. RIANA HAND REARS THE ABANDONED OR ORPHANED ANIMALS AND USES THEM TO RAISE AWARENESS OF ENDANGERED SPECIES IN HER COUNTRY.

Riana with the latest addition to her cat family, baby cheetah Aviva.

Fiela, who shares 55 lb (25 kg) of chicken a day with the other animals, is seen here sitting at the dinner table with her owner Riana.

Riana bought her first cheetah, Fiela, in 2006 at just six weeks old. Fiela is fully house-trained and allowed to roam free in Riana's house.

℞ CHEMICAL ALERT

Argentine ants produce chemicals that alert their nestmates to the fact that they are still alive. Once they stop producing it, they are picked up and carried to a garbage pile by the other ants.

℞ FLAG THIEF

A squirrel was caught stealing small U.S. flags from a cemetery and carrying them up to its nest. Every Memorial Day, volunteers place the flags next to the graves of nearly 1,000 veterans buried at Mount Hope Cemetery in Port Huron, Michigan, but in May 2009, workers noticed several flags had been torn off their wooden staffs. The cheeky squirrel was then spotted detaching a flag and running up a tree with it to the nest.

℞ LEG TWITCH

A harvestman arachnid's legs can twitch for up to an hour after being detached from its body.

℞ PIGEON HONOR

G.I. Joe, a carrier pigeon for the U.S. Army, helped save the lives of 1,000 British soldiers during World War II—and in 1946, London's mayor presented him with an honorary medal for his work.

℞ LARGE APPETITE

Indonesia's Komodo dragons, the world's largest lizards, can weigh more than 170 lb (77 kg) and are capable of eating 80 percent of their body weight in a single meal.

℞ NAME CHECK

Smokey the cockatiel was reunited with his owner after saying his own name on the phone. Having escaped from the home of David Edwards, the missing bird had been found in nearby Wrexham, North Wales. To prove that she was the rightful owner, Mrs. Edwards asked for Smokey to be put on the phone and as soon as he heard her voice, he started repeating his name.

℞ WHO'S A CLEVER BOY?

In 2009, the American Red Cross presented an award to Willie the parrot for saving the life of two-year-old Hannah Kuusk at her home in Denver, Colorado. When Hannah started choking on some food, the normally quiet Willie alerted his owner by flapping his wings and repeatedly squawking, "Momma, Baby!"

℞ SWALLOWED WHOLE

An Australian woman was horrified when her pet dog was swallowed whole by a snake in March 2009. Patty Buntine of Katherine, Northern Territory, was worried when Bindi, her three-year-old Maltese terrier cross, went missing. On going outside to investigate, she saw the snake with its belly bulging so much it was unable to move. The dog amounted to around 60 percent of the snake's bodyweight, which meant that the serpent's snack was like a fully grown man swallowing a 16-year-old boy.

℞ EXPLODING GLANDS

Several species of Southeast Asian ants have exploding glands in their heads, allowing them to launch suicidal chemical attacks on enemies.

℞ SYNTHETIC BEAK

A stork with a damaged beak was given a new one in 2009 by a Hungarian bird hospital. The stork, which was thought to have flown into a wall, had its lower beak repaired in an operation, while specialist Tamas Kothay built a new top beak out of synthetic resin.

Snake Attack

A python was caught suffocating an unfortunate cockatoo in Cairns, Australia, in 2008. Artist Cindy Lane was working in her studio when she heard loud squawking, and moving outside she discovered the snake coiling itself around the bird high up in a tree in her backyard. She reported that the python took around two hours to completely swallow its feathered prey.

ACTUAL SIZE!

Flappy Meal

A GOLDEN ORB WEAVER SPIDER MANAGED TO ENSNARE A CHESTNUT–BREASTED MANNIKIN FINCH IN ITS WEB IN A GARDEN NEAR ATHERTON, AUSTRALIA. THE GIANT SPIDER WOULD HAVE THEN PROCEEDED TO INJECT THE STRUGGLING BIRD WITH VENOM TO PREPARE IT FOR EATING, AND WRAP THE CORPSE INTO A FOOD PARCEL, AS IT WOULD BE TOO MUCH FOR THE SPIDER TO EAT IN ONE SITTING. GOLDEN ORB WEAVER SPIDERS CAN GROW LARGER THAN A HUMAN HAND AND USUALLY PREY ON LARGE INSECTS, SO IT IS HIGHLY UNUSUAL TO SEE ONE CATCHING A BIRD.

℞ HIGH LIFE

The common swift spends most of its life in flight, nests on vertical surfaces, and never willingly touches the ground.

℞ DANCING PARROT

The antics of a cockatoo from Indiana on an Internet video-sharing website have convinced scientists that birds really do dance to music. More than two million people viewed Snowball's rhythmic movements online as his dancing feet diligently followed the beat of his favorite Backstreet Boys song, even when the tune was speeded up or slowed down.

℞ FEATHERED CRITICS

By rewarding them with food, Japanese scientists believe that racing pigeons can be trained to study paintings and evaluate them—exactly as you might expect from an art critic. The study shows that, with practice, pigeons can learn to appreciate the color, pattern, and texture of paintings.

℞ WOLF DETERRENT

Wolves can be kept at bay using a simple technique of a rope with a red ribbon, or series of red flags, tied to it. The technique is known as fladry and has been used for centuries in Europe.

℞ DARING DIVE

To impress a mate, Anna's hummingbird (named after a 19th-century Italian duchess called Anna Massena) dives through the air at speeds of around 50 mph (80 km/h). Sometimes the dives are aimed at other birds, sometimes at people. Because the bird is typically only 4 in (10 cm) long, its speed is the equivalent of a car traveling at 1,300 mph (2,090 km/h)—that's almost twice the speed of sound. To perform its astonishing dive, the tiny hummingbird—a native of California— must whirl its wings at more than 1,000 beats a minute and burn body fuel some 400 times faster than a human.

ANGRY HIPPOS

A CROCODILE WAS BITTEN TO DEATH AFTER BECOMING TRAPPED AMONG A GANG OF 50 ANGRY HIPPOS ON THE BANKS OF THE GRUMETI RIVER IN THE SERENGETI NATIONAL PARK, TANZANIA. THE CROC GOT TOO CLOSE TO A FEMALE HIPPO AND HER CALVES, AND THE ENTIRE HIPPO GROUP GATHERED IN A CIRCLE TO PROTECT THEM. INSTEAD OF BACKING OFF, THE CROC PANICKED AND TRIED TO ESCAPE ACROSS THE BACKS OF THE HIPPOS, WHO RESPONDED WITH A FRENZIED ATTACK. THE CROC'S ARMOR-PLATED BODY WAS NO MATCH FOR THE HIPPOS' HUGE TEETH, WHICH CAN APPLY SEVERAL TONS OF PRESSURE IN A SINGLE BITE. FIGHTS BETWEEN HIPPOS AND CROCS ARE RARE, AS THEY USUALLY SHOW MUTUAL RESPECT, BUT WHEN A HIPPO HAS YOUNG TO PROTECT, IT BECOMES ONE OF THE MOST AGGRESSIVE CREATURES IN THE ANIMAL KINGDOM.

® BEEHIVE FENCE

Farmers in Kenya stop elephants from destroying food crops by using fences of bees to frighten the animals away. The fences are constructed of beehives connected by lengths of wire, and while the elephants manage to avoid the hives, their efforts to force their way through the wire cause the hives to swing violently and the bees to attack. The angry bees swarm around the elephants' eyes and up their trunks and can even kill elephant calves because they have thinner hides than adult elephants.

® MANY TEETH

While humans get only two sets of natural teeth to last them their entire life, alligators get between 2,000 and 3,000 teeth during their lifetime.

® TALENTED TERRIERS

When dog owner Sun Chien of Shenyang, China, suffered a stroke, he built a shopping cart and trained his two terriers—Pong Pong and Wow Wow—to do his shopping. The dogs push the cart, which has holders for money and shopping lists, to the shops by themselves—and if one gets tired, he hops in and lets the other one do the pushing for a while.

SHARK CESAREAN

When a pregnant shark at an aquarium in Auckland, New Zealand, was bitten in the side by another shark, visitors watched in amazement as four baby sharks swam out through the gaping wound. Staff described the deep gouge as like the mother shark having a cesarean section. The injured shark needed stitches—but only after four more pups were found alive inside her.

® BABY SAVED

A dog was believed to have saved the life of an abandoned baby girl in La Plata, Argentina, in 2008 by keeping her warm with her own puppies. Farmer Fabio Anze found the naked baby girl, who was just a few hours old, among his dog China's puppies.

® FROG'S LEG

A giant bullfrog that had been attacked by a dog near Johannesburg, South Africa, became the first frog in the world to be fitted with a false leg. In a delicate two-hour operation, the amphibian had his shattered lower leg bone replaced with a one-inch-long (2.5-cm) steel rod.

® BARBECUE HORROR

A Chihuahua puppy survived after spending three days with a barbecue fork embedded in his brain. Twelve-week-old Smokey was playing at a family barbecue in London, Kentucky, in 2009 when a fork snapped in half on the grill, flew through the air, and impaled itself in his head. The dog ran off into nearby trees but was found cowering in the undergrowth two days later and taken to an animal hospital where the 3-in (8-cm) prongs were removed from his brain.

® HOLY COW

A calf born in a remote village in Pursat Province, Cambodia, in August 2009 had thick, dark, scaly skin like a crocodile's. The day after it was born, a three-month drought ended, leading villagers to declare the calf to be holy. The animal lived for only three days, but was given a ceremonial funeral.

® BIONIC GOOSE

When a two-week-old gosling was found with a broken leg, veterinarians at Tiggywinkles Wildlife Hospital, Buckinghamshire, England, gave the little bird a bionic limb. She was fitted with tiny steel pins, nuts, and bolts to build a leg brace that enabled her to walk again.

ACKNOWLEDGMENTS

COVER (t) Zak-n-Wheezie hatched on 6/14/07 to Frank and Barbara Witte of www.fresnodragons.com, (c) Picture by Ian McLelland on behalf of PDSA, (b) Todd Mecklem; 4 Picture by Ian McLelland on behalf of PDSA; 6 (t, b) Cardoso Flea Circus, by Maria Fernanda Cardoso Produced by the Fabric Workshop and Museum, Philadelphia. Collection of the Tate Gallery London. Photo credits: Ross Rudesch Harley; 6–7 (b/r-t/r) © Bettmann/Corbis; 7 (t) © Nicole Duplaix/Corbis, (c) © Hulton-Deutsch Collection/Corbis, (b/l) Hannah Grace Deller /Starstock/Photoshot, (b/r) © Bettmann/Corbis; 8 (t) Barcroft Media Ltd, (b) Bournemouth News/Rex Features; 9 Zak-n-Wheezie hatched on 6/14/07 to Frank and Barbara Witte of www.fresnodragons.com; 10 (t) Todd Mecklem, (b) Wenn.com; 11 Picture by Ian McLelland on behalf of PDSA; 12 Wenn.com; 13 (t) Caters News Agency Ltd/Rex Features, (b) Gary Florin/Rex Features; 14 (t) Jung von Matt/Neckar, (b) Melissa Smith; 15 Brendan Beckett/Barcroft Media Ltd; 16 Keith Ringland; 17 (b) Drew Fitzgibbon/Newspix/Rex Features; (t) © NHPA/Photoshot; 18 Eric Cheng/Barcroft Media Ltd; 19 (t) ChinaFotoPress/Photocome/Press Association Images, (b) Heng Sinith/AP/Press Association Images; 20 (t/l) Dana Fineman Courtesy of The Venice Beach Freakshow, (t/r) Priscilla Cermeno-Shakur, (b) Dana Fineman Courtesy of The Venice Beach Freakshow; 21 (b, c/r, b/l, b/r) Dana Fineman Courtesy of The Venice Beach Freakshow, (t/r, c/l) Asia Ray Courtesy of The Venice Beach Freakshow; 22 (t) Apichart Weerawong/AP/Press Association Images, (b) Barry Bland/Barcroft Media Ltd; 23 www.redfernnaturalhistory.com; 24 (t) © EuroPics[CEN], (b) Caters News; 26 © UPPA/Photoshot; 27 (t) Reuters/Cathal McNaughton, (b) Martin Birchall/Rex Features; 28 (t) Rex Features, (b) Chris Ison/PA Archive/Press Association Images; 29 Caters News Agency Ltd/Rex Features; 30 Cindy Lane/Newspix/Rex Features; 31 Newspix/Rex Features; 32 Vaclav Silha/Barcroft USA Ltd; 33 Kelly Tarltons Underwater World; BACK COVER Jung von Matt/Neckar

Key: t = top, b = bottom, c = center, l = left, r = right, sp = single page, dp = double page

All other photos are from Ripley Entertainment Inc.
Every attempt has been made to acknowledge correctly and contact copyright holders and we apologize in advance for any unintentional errors or omissions, which will be corrected in future editions.